WILD WHEELS!

Hottest NASCAR Machines

By K.C. Kelley

E | **Enslow Publishers, Inc.**
40 Industrial Road
Box 398
Berkeley Heights, NJ 07922
USA

http://www.enslow.com

Library of Congress Cataloging-in-Publication Data

Kelley, K. C.
  Hottest NASCAR machines / by K.C. Kelley.
    p. cm. — (Wild wheels!)
  Summary: "Experience the thrill of a NASCAR race, and learn about the cars,
personalities, and races associated with this sport"—Provided by publisher.
  Includes bibliographical references and index.
  ISBN-13: 978-0-7660-2869-2 (library edition)
  ISBN-10: 0-7660-2869-0 (library edition)
  1. NASCAR (Association)—History—Juvenile literature. 2. Stock car
racing—United States—History—Juvenile literature. 3. Stock
cars—Juvenile literature. I. Title.
  GV1029.9.S74K454 2008
  796.72—dc22   2007007426

ISBN-13: 978-0-7760-3610-9 (paperback)
ISBN-10: 0-7760-3610-3 (paperback)

Printed in the United States of America

10 9 8 7 6 5 4

To Our Readers: We have done our best to make sure that all Internet Addresses in this
book were active and appropriate when we went to press. However, the author and
publisher have no control over and assume no liability for the material available on those
Internet sites or on other Web sites they may link to. Any comments or suggestions can be
sent by e-mail to comments@enslow.com or to the address on the back cover.

Disclaimer: This publication is not affiliated with, endorsed by, or sponsored by NASCAR.
NASCAR®, WINSTON CUP®, NEXTEL CUP, BUSCH SERIES and CRAFTSMAN
TRUCK SERIES are trademarks owned or controlled by the National Association for
Stock Car Auto Racing, Inc., and are registered where indicated.

Cover photo: Wayne Keister/Motorace Graphiks **Back cover:** AP/David Graham

Photo Credits: Alamy/Wesley Hitt, p. 8; Alamy/Transtock Inc., p. 11; AP/Charlie Berch,
p. 38; AP/Chuck Burton, pp. 18 top, 18 bottom, 24; AP/Ric Feld, p. 43 bottom; AP/David
Graham, pp. 3, 22–23; AP/Carolyn Kaster, p. 19 bottom; AP/Robert E. Klein, pp. 1, 16;
AP/Donald Miralle/Allsport, pp. 1, 43 top; AP/Chris O'Meara, pp. 3, 4–5, 32; AP/John
Raoux, p. 31; Associated Press/AP, p. 9; Todd Corzette, p. 13; Getty Images/Jonathan Ferrey,
p. 35 bottom; Getty Images/Darrell Ingham, p. 28; Getty Images/Robert Laberge, p. 26;
Getty Images/Streeter Lecka, p. 35 middle; Getty Images/Donald Miralle, pp. 12, 36; Getty
Images/Thomas Raymond/Stone, p. 30; Mary & Andy McGavic, pp. 1, 14, 20, 27 top &
bottom; Motorace Graphiks/Cathy Keister, p. 39; Motorace Graphiks/Ade Ketchum, pp. 3,
40, 42; Motorsports Image and Archives Photography, pp. 3, 35 top; Pro30 Racing, Inc., pp.
3, 15, 41; State Archives of Florida, p. 7; Ware Racing Enterprises, p. 19 top, 19 center.

Contents

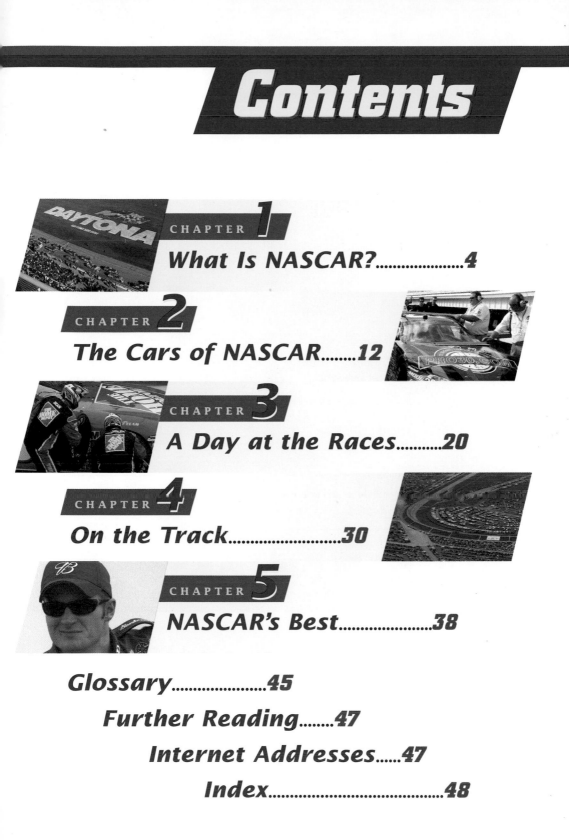

CHAPTER 1

What Is NASCAR?

Under a hot Florida sun at the Daytona International Speedway, the noise is incredible—from the powerful roar of 43 mighty engines and from hundreds of thousands of cheering fans. The speed is intense—cars fly around the 2.5-mile track at nearly 200 miles per hour! The 2007 Daytona 500, the most famous of the dozens of NASCAR races held each year, is nearing its end. Both the fans and the drivers are waiting eagerly for the checkered flag to drop—and the winner to cross the finish line!

The colorful, powerful cars drive around the final turn, bumper to bumper, inches apart while moving at amazing speeds. Drivers battle for position, testing their nerves and skills to gain a split second or a few inches. The finish line is just ahead and one car pulls out in front. The checkered flag waves overhead as the car passes by. At that moment, a huge roar erupts from the crowd and the race is over. The winner, driver Kevin Harvick in the Number 29 car, winds down during a victory lap. This Daytona 500 is over. The sights and sounds of the day are seared into the memories of the millions watching in person and on television.

Becoming the Number-One Sport

Since the early 1990s, the National Association for Stock Car Auto Racing (NASCAR) has shot upward in popularity. In some parts of the United States, it is the number-one sport. The drivers have become national heroes, while the races draw enormous crowds and huge TV audiences at tracks from coast to coast.

It was not always like that. NASCAR began in the Deep South in the late 1930s and early 1940s. Fast-car fans began to gather at small, local dirt tracks, and as those races grew in size, some of the track owners and drivers decided that getting organized would be a good idea.

In 1948 in Daytona Beach, Florida, William "Big Bill" France, a local driver, gathered all the top drivers together and they created NASCAR, a new organization to help their sport grow.

Today's drivers earn millions of dollars (the winner's prize at some top races can be more than $1 million), but none of the early NASCAR drivers earned their living just by racing. For some, their racing cars were the same ones they used to take the family to the store or to the movies. Drivers would sometimes just paint their car number on the side and head to the track. They drove

Racing fans gather at Daytona Beach, Florida, to watch a race in the late 1940s. This was around the time NASCAR was started.

"stock cars," which was another term for regular passenger cars.

Once at the track, the drivers were often their own mechanics, or brought along friends and family to help. They had to bring their own gas and gear, change their own tires, and fix anything that went wrong. Today's drivers have teams of

Meet the King!

Richard Petty is the most successful NASCAR driver of all time. He grew up around race cars. Petty's father, Lee, was one of the sport's early stars.

By the mid–1960s, the younger Petty was the best driver on the circuit. He won his first season title in 1964. In 1967, he won an astounding 27 races, still a single-year record. Around this time, Petty earned his nickname: "The King."

Petty won seven NASCAR championships, the most ever until the great Dale Earnhardt, Sr., tied that mark in 1994. When Petty retired in 1992, he had won an all-time record 200 races. Only one other racer, David Pearson, has won even half that many, with 105.

Petty remains involved in NASCAR as a team owner, and his son Kyle is a NASCAR driver. But while there have been other Pettys on the track, there will always be only one King.

dozens of people helping them out, on and off the track.

Early Heroes and New Tracks

Like today's drivers, the early driving heroes loved one thing more than anything else: driving fast. Lee Petty was an early hero, as were Curtis Turner and Herb Thomas. The Flock family of Alabama also featured several successful drivers. In one race, Tim, Fonty, and Bob Flock were joined at the starting line by their sister Ethel. They steered their big, heavy cars around dusty tracks at speeds above 100 miles per hour (mph). They were never afraid to bump into an opponent to gain an advantage in a tight race.

Early NASCAR driver Fonty Flock before a race in Daytona, Florida, in 1956.

By the middle of the 1950s, NASCAR had grown. As more fans began to head to the racetracks to watch, more tracks were built. The first large paved oval track opened at Darlington, South Carolina, in 1950. In 1959,

Bill France opened Daytona International Speedway. Before this superspeedway came along, cars raced at about 110 to 120 mph. But with the size of this track they could achieve speeds of 150 mph and above, which meant more exciting races.

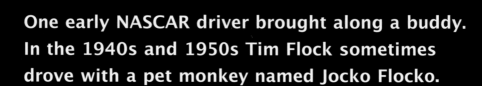

WILD FACT

One early NASCAR driver brought along a buddy. In the 1940s and 1950s Tim Flock sometimes drove with a pet monkey named Jocko Flocko.

NASCAR continued to grow bigger and bigger. Tracks were built in states such as California and New Hampshire—far away from NASCAR's roots in the South. Stars like Richard Petty, David Pearson, Cale Yarborough, and Ned Jarrett became champions and heroes. In the 1980s, races began to be covered regularly by live TV. NASCAR reached an even wider audience. In the 1990s, NASCAR finally became one of America's top sports.

NASCAR Today

The top level of NASCAR racing is currently called the Nextel Cup, after its major sponsor. Drivers in the Nextel Cup earn points for their finishing position in each race and for such things as most laps led in a race. After the first 26 races, drivers in the top ten in points enter a special competition. In the next ten races, those ten drivers can earn additional points. These final ten races are known as the "Chase" for the season championship. After the final race, the driver with the most points is the NASCAR Nextel Cup champion.

Another division of NASCAR racing is the Busch Series, which can be a proving ground for drivers who are preparing to step up to the Nextel Cup series.

NASCAR also organizes the Craftsman Truck Series, where specially modified pickup trucks race on many of the same ovals as Nextel and Busch cars. Below these are several regional series held on smaller tracks. Drivers on these circuits hope to impress the team owners at higher levels. These circuits are the "minor leagues" of stock car racing.

The stock cars of NASCAR are based on regular cars. This one, in a spinout with Kurt Busch at the wheel, is based on a Ford Taurus.

CHAPTER 2

The Cars of NASCAR

Can just anyone head out to a local car dealership and pick up a NASCAR vehicle? The answer is no—but they can buy one that looks like the body of a NASCAR vehicle, such as a Dodge Charger, Ford Fusion, or Toyota Tundra truck. The exterior designs of all the vehicles raced in NASCAR are based on models sold to everyday drivers. But that is where the similarity ends. All NASCAR vehicles are designed especially for racing.

From front to rear, a Nextel Cup car is packed with special features that turn these stock cars into super-fast racing cars.

Engine

The powerhouse that makes a Nextel Cup car go is a 358-cubic-inch V-8. This engine is about 30 to 40 percent larger than the engine in a typical passenger car. "V-8" means that it has eight pistons, arranged in a V-shape. These move up and down rapidly

Every Nextel Cup car is powered by a big, powerful V-8 engine like this one.

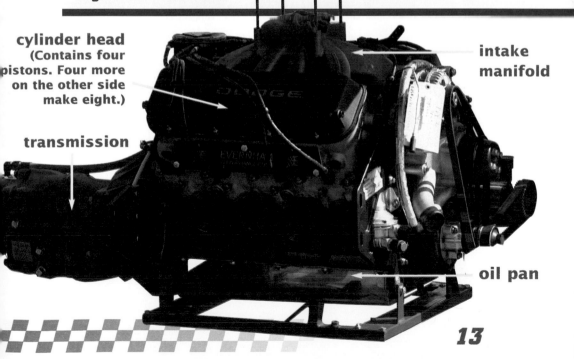

cylinder head
(Contains four pistons. Four more on the other side make eight.)

intake manifold

transmission

oil pan

to turn the driveshaft, which helps to turn the wheels.

This engine can produce 850 horsepower (hp). Horsepower is a measure of engine performance, comparing the power created by one horse to what the engine can do. This means it would take 850 horses working together to produce enough power to drive a Nextel Cup car at top speed!

WILD

FACT

The "headlights" on a Nextel Cup car are not real lights—they are just decals (stickers)! Lights are not needed on a racetrack. They also break easily, leaving debris and causing a safety issue on the track.

Chassis

Designed with the help of computers, wind tunnels, and endless testing, the chassis (CHASS-ee) is like the skeleton of the car. It is

NASCAR officials measure every part of a car before giving it the "OK" to race.

made of thick steel tubes welded together. It is designed to be strong enough to protect the driver as well as to support the heavy engine.

Body

The shape of a Nextel Cup car is carefully controlled by NASCAR officials. All teams must use the same body types, and for each body type, the cars must be built exactly the same. Officials use special measuring devices to make sure all teams are using the same shape of a certain car. Why all the rules? Because a car's shape affects how it moves through the air. That can greatly affect how fast it goes. Making sure that all the cars move the same way puts the emphasis on engine performance and driver skill.

Cockpit

The driver's compartment is called the cockpit. There is room for only one person in this car—there are no back seats. On the dashboard in front of the driver are switches and gauges. They help the driver control parts of the car, and also let him see

The driver's cockpit is packed with all the instruments needed to keep track of engine performance during a race.

such things as how hot the engine is and how much power is in the battery. The steering wheel is much smaller than in a regular passenger car. It is easily removable, too. This allows the driver to climb into and out of the seat, which is very close to the steering wheel.

Next to the steering wheel is the gear shift lever. Having different gears helps car engines move more safely to higher speeds. Without gears, car engines would overheat very quickly by powering up too fast.

Finally, a radio button is located on the steering wheel. The radio, which includes earphones and a helmet microphone, allows the driver to communicate with his pit crew.

Accessories

There are not many! Nextel Cup cars have no doors—drivers climb in through window openings. There are no side windows, only netting. There is no speedometer, either—the driver must figure out the car's speed by reading the engine revolutions per minute (rpm's). And, of course, there is no stereo system. It would be too loud in the car to hear music, anyway!

How to Make a NASCAR Race Car

Building a new NASCAR race car from scratch takes dozens of people and many hours. There are several steps involved in creating a NASCAR race car:

Using computer models, a chassis is built. The heavy steel tubes at the front

of the car will hold the engine in place. The bars that surround the driver's cockpit are the roll cage. The wider panels on the side offer more protection for the driver.

A body made of sheet metal and high-tech fiberglass is placed over the chassis. The body's shape is created using wind-tunnel testing and computer modeling based on NASCAR

rules. The front spindles and rear axles (which hold the wheels) and brakes have been installed.

Inside the car, the driver's seat and instrument panel have been put in. The wheels and body are attached to the chassis, and then it is time for painting. Grey "primer" paint is applied. The windshield is also added now.

One of the final steps is to apply paint and designs to the car. The car's colors depend on the team's major sponsor. Then, dozens of other sponsors' decals are attached, along with "headlight" stickers. The driver's name is usually painted on the roof over the door.

While one part of the team works on the car's chassis and body, another is creating the engine. Hours of testing are done on each of the engine's hundreds of parts. Finally, the engine is built and it is lowered into the car. Wires, cables, belts, and hoses attach the engine to all the car's systems.

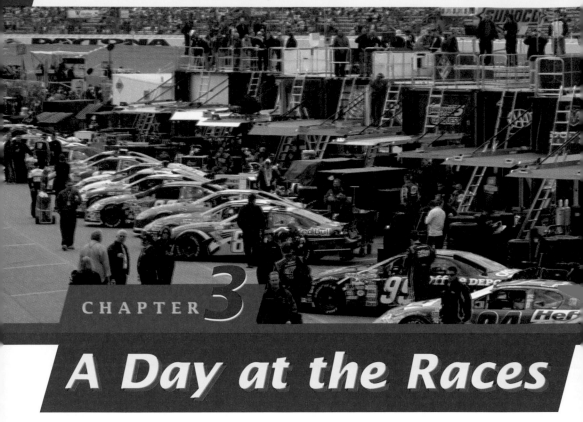

CHAPTER 3

A Day at the Races

A NASCAR race day is colorful, noisy, crowded—and for real fans, a little slice of heaven. At tracks around the country, a typical Sunday race draws more than 100,000 fans. Larger tracks such as Daytona or Talladega (in Alabama) regularly see crowds of more than 200,000 people. They fill the stands that surround the track and also cover the infield (the central area inside the track).

Race weekend starts Thursday or Friday for most NASCAR teams. Crews spend the day unloading cars, engines, tools, spare parts, and other gear. Drivers usually run practice laps in their race cars, in front of empty stands that will soon be filled with cheering fans.

Qualifying is often held on Friday afternoon or Saturday morning. To determine the starting order of the race, each driver runs a certain number of qualifying laps, depending on the track. The drivers with the highest speeds will get the best starting positions for the race, near the front of the field. NASCAR races start with 21 rows of two cars each, with one car in a final row. This forms a 43-car starting "grid."

Crews then go over their cars inch by inch, making tiny adjustments based on computer tests and driver input. They might tighten the steering or adjust the balance of the wheels, all in an effort to coax every last bit of speed out their car.

The Races Begin

Friday and Saturday are when many fans start to arrive. Hundreds drive their motor homes onto the infield, where they

The Pit Crew

Drivers make several pit stops during every race to get new tires put on their cars and to get refueled. Each of the seven pit crew members has a particular job. The best crews can change four tires and fill the gas tank in about 13 to 15 seconds!

Catch-can man: This crew member uses a catch-can to catch any excess fuel that overflows from the car. He or she also takes the first emptied gas can from the gas man so a second can of fuel can be put into the car.

Gas man: Wearing special fire-resistant clothes, the gas man pours gas into the valve at the rear of the car.

will spend the weekend barbecuing, seeing friends, and watching the race up close.

Saturday of race weekend often means a Busch Series race at the track. For the Busch drivers, this is the highlight of their weekend. If they do well in these races, they may catch the eye of team owners looking for drivers to move up to the Nextel Cup series.

With the Nextel cars fine-tuned and the drivers rested and ready, Sunday dawns—race

Tire carriers: These two crew members carry the 80-pound tires to their new places and hang them after they remove the old tires.

Tire changers: With air-powered wrenches, these two members of the pit crew remove the five lug nuts that hold each tire in place. They then put five new nuts on the new tire after it is hung by the tire carriers.

Jack man: Using a large car jack, the jack man lifts the car so the tires can be changed.

day. Drivers attend a morning safety meeting with track officials to go over the day's routine and rules. Crews are busy readying the car for the starting grid. To save gas and to prevent extra wear and tear on engines, the cars are pushed, not driven, into their places on the starting grid on pit road.

At many tracks, the drivers are introduced one by one on a stage. A stage set up at the start-finish line might be as much as a mile away from fans on the other side of the track, so large video screens help them keep up with the action and ceremonies.

After driver introductions, drivers stand by their cars while crews line pit road, their uniforms forming a rainbow of colors 43 teams strong. The national anthem and other music is performed. At some races, military jets roar by just overhead, their engines challenging the sound about to erupt from the race cars.

Cars and drivers are lined up on pit road before a race at Lowe's Motor Speedway in Concord, North Carolina, in 2006.

Officials at the start–finish line wave flags to indicate events during a race. Different flags mean different things:

START racing! Or start again after a stoppage or slowdown.

Take CAUTION. Everyone must slow down to the same speed after a crash to let debris (broken car parts) be cleared from the track.

STOP! All cars must stop, and go to an area determined by a NASCAR official. The race might be stopped for sudden bad weather or other emergencies.

Busted! A rule has been broken. The driver or team that broke the rule must go to its pit stall to wait out a PENALTY of one or more laps.

Slower drivers who are a lap or more behind are about to be passed by faster cars. They must MOVE OUT OF THE WAY and let the faster cars pass safely.

It is the LAST LAP of the race.

The END OF THE RACE! This is the flag every driver wants to see first. It is waved when the winner crosses the finish line.

Start Your Engines!

Soon the drivers hear the most famous words in car racing: "Start your engines!" The drivers push a button that sends their mighty engines roaring to life. Forty-three 850-hp blocks of iron blast their sound into the air. The race is just minutes away.

The pace car roars out onto the track, and the cars in the starting grid leave pit road and follow slowly along. NASCAR races

The yellow pace car gets all the cars driving at the same speed before a race at Arizona's Phoenix International Raceway in 2006.

Race Day Supplies

Each NASCAR team has an 18-wheeler, called a hauler, loaded with gear that they move from track to track. For a weekend of racing, a team has an amazing amount of gear in their trailer:

- two or three race cars
- spare car body parts
- an extra engine
- virtually every engine part
- hundreds of tools of all sorts
- clothing for all the crew members

Goodyear provides tires to each team. Most teams also have several motor homes that are used by the driver and crew members at the track, as a place to rest and eat meals. It is like moving an entire garage and a car dealership in a weekend!

use a rolling start, that is, the race begins while the cars are already moving. The pace car "sets the pace," letting all the cars get up to the same speed. The pace car leads the field for a number of laps, then quickly peels into pit road to get out of the way. As the cars reach the starting line on the third

Officials in White

On the side of the track and in the pits, TV viewers might see people in white jumpsuits, often wearing racing helmets. These are not drivers looking for their rides—they are NASCAR officials. Dozens of officials work each race, supervising pit crews, mechanics, and drivers to make sure that all rules are followed. They have the power to hold a car in the pits for doing something wrong or to report violations to top race officials for later penalties.

pace lap, the green flag drops and, in a heartbeat, the cars are almost flying down the track, heading into the first turn.

If you have ever been near a jet engine when it takes off, you know the feeling of having your insides wiggle and vibrate with the force of the sound. That is what it is like at the start of a NASCAR race—and it goes on like that for hours!

During the race, fans can keep track of the action, as well as their favorite drivers, by buying special headphones on which they can hear track announcers. They also view video screens and look at the scoring towers, to see the always-changing order of the cars in the race.

The action speeds up and slows down, depending on caution laps (when an accident stops or slows the action on the track) and pit stops (when cars stop in pit stalls to get new tires and more gas). But most of the time it is all-out racing. Few events in sports are as emotionally powerful and physically draining as a NASCAR race. If you ever get the chance to go, grab it—and bring your earplugs!

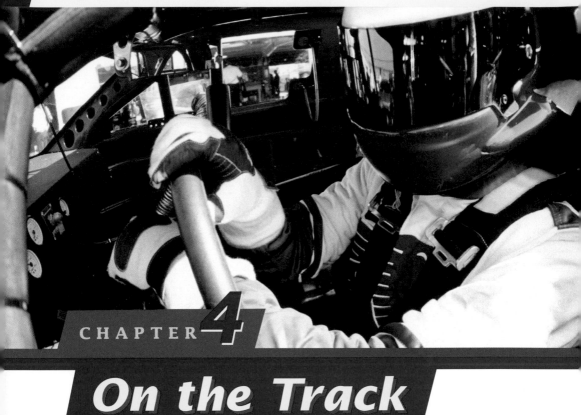

CHAPTER 4

On the Track

Driving a NASCAR vehicle is easy, right? You just climb in, strap on your helmet, put the pedal to the metal and turn left for three hours. Not exactly! It is more complicated than that. There is much more going on inside the cockpit . . . and under the helmet.

The driver is strapped tightly into the seat, hands gripping the steering wheel. As the green flag drops, the driver stomps on the gas pedal, quickly shifting through the gears to reach top speed. The noise is incredible, but the driver's ears are protected by a thick helmet and earplugs. The vibration, however, is something the driver just has to get used to. At the speeds these cars are moving, every little bump on the track, or from another car, rattles through the nearly padless car.

Drivers have to cope with temperatures as high as 120 degrees. Their boots are lined with heat-resistant material, since the heat from the engine can sometimes melt the rubber soles. They get no meal breaks, no bathroom breaks, and no time outs. They might get something to drink during a pit stop, but that is all.

Driver Jeff Gordon takes time to adjust his boot before a qualifying run at the 2007 Daytona 500.

Some people argue that race car drivers are not real athletes. Those people have never spent four hours muscling a 3,400-pound race car around a track while bathed in sweat.

Early NASCAR vehicles had almost no safety gear. Today's cars are packed with it!

- The cockpit is surrounded by a steel **roll cage** that protects the driver in a crash.

- The **seat** is form-fit for the driver's body, so that he or she does not rock around during a race or a crash.

Dale Earnhardt, Jr., puts on his helmet and HANS device.

- The driver wears a heavy-duty **seat belt** that goes around both shoulders and both legs.

- The driver's helmet includes a set of cables and braces. This is a **head and neck support (HANS) device**. It keeps the head from whipping forward or sideways in a crash, which can cause serious injury.

- The front **windshield** is made of plastic that is nearly unbreakable. When it does break, it crumbles, rather than shattering into sharp pieces.

- **Roof flaps** on top of the car open if the car suddenly turns backward. This helps prevent it from flipping over.

- Some cars have a **rooftop hatch** through which drivers can exit quickly in an emergency.

The drivers are battling the heat and noise, not to mention the other drivers. The goal is to get in front of the pack. The ability to use speed, daring, and split-second timing to pass other drivers is the key to NASCAR success.

WILD FACT

Just how hot does it get inside a race car? In the 1980s a television crew shot pictures of an egg frying on the floor of Cale Yarborough's car!

Drivers can go "high," meaning toward the outside of the track, but must then fight the car, which wants to keep going higher. Drivers can also go "low," toward the inside of the track, but must be able to hold the car in a tight turn at high speed. They can also use a technique called "drafting." Drafting is following very closely behind another car. By keeping their car just inches behind another car, drivers can give their engines a bit of a break. The car in front is "cutting through" the air, making the second car's ride smoother. Drivers make dozens of these decisions every moment during a race.

They also watch up ahead. A puff of smoke half a mile up the track might mean an accident, so drivers must be ready to avoid trouble quickly. They want to do this without reducing their speed, if possible. They are also on the radio with their crews, figuring out when they should come in for a pit stop.

In the Pit

When it is time for a pit stop, a driver enters pit road from the main track. The car slows almost instantly from more than 150 mph to as little as 30 mph, depending on the track. The driver parks the car, engine running, in its pit stall. Then, like an army of ants, the team's pit crew scrambles around the car, changing tires and filling the gas tank. They might also clean the windshield, give the driver water, or make minor adjustments to the car. Just seconds later, the driver roars out of the pit area and back onto the track, steering into the race.

Around and around they go, for hundreds of miles and laps, for as long as three or four

Types of Tracks

NASCAR races are held on several types of tracks. The tracks are of different lengths, and the races held on them range from 350 to 600 miles. The name of a race often tells the length of the race, such as the Daytona 500 (500 miles). The length of the race determines how many laps around the track the drivers must go.

Talladega Superspeedway

Superspeedway: An oval track of 2.5 miles or longer. For NASCAR races, only Daytona in Florida and Talladega in Alabama fall into this category.

Intermediate: An oval track of 1.0 to 2.5 miles. Most NASCAR tracks are in this category.

Short track: An oval track of less than one-half mile. Bristol in Tennessee and Martinsville in Virginia are examples.

Martinsville Speedway

Sears Point Raceway

Road course: A longer, twisting, narrower track. There are dozens of NASCAR road courses, but Watkins Glen in New York and Sears Point in California are the only two Nextel Cup courses.

hours. One of the hardest parts of being a driver is staying focused for that long. If drivers stop paying close attention for just a moment, they might find themselves spinning out in the infield, into a wall, and

Pit crews work furiously refueling cars and changing tires during the Food City 500 at Bristol Motor Speedway in Tennessee.

How to Become a NASCAR Driver

New NASCAR drivers do not just show up at the track, ready to race at the Nextel Cup level. They have to work their way up through other types of racing. Many start out in go-karts, which are low-slung, high-powered cars that can be raced by kids as young as five years old. They might move up to sports cars or "midget" cars, which are smaller and raced on short tracks, often on dirt.

Other drivers learn their skills racing off-road in deserts, on motorcycles, or in trucks. Local quarter-mile asphalt tracks are another place that younger drivers learn the tricks of the trade. All of their driving experience is examined by team owners. If an owner thinks the driver has the skills to help the team, the driver might get a shot at a Busch Series race. Success there can mean a "promotion" to the top level, the Nextel Cup.

perhaps losing the race. At the speeds they are moving, they cover a distance equal to the length of a football field in just a couple of seconds!

As the race nears its end, the bumping and drafting gets more intense as the leaders fight for position. Finally, the checkered flag flies over the winner's car.

CHAPTER 5

NASCAR's Best

NASCAR drivers are among the sports world's most beloved figures. Fans follow their favorites with great loyalty, and buy tens of millions of dollars' worth of souvenirs.

Some have even named their children after their favorites! It is not unusual to see fans sporting tattoos of their favorite drivers' names and car numbers.

Several of the most popular drivers today are champions, and all expect to be competing every fall during the Chase for the Nextel Cup.

His fans hope that Jeff Gordon will win another Nextel Cup championship and stay in the lead.

Jeff Gordon: Gordon is second all-time in NASCAR championships with four (behind the seven of both Richard Petty and Dale Earnhardt, Sr.), but his last championship was in 2001. Gordon remains a top contender, however. He had 73 career race victories leading into the 2007 season. His 33 wins since 1999 are the most in that time. He also has won more money as a driver than anyone else in NASCAR history—more than $56 million!

Tony Stewart: A two-time NASCAR champion, Stewart is used to titles. He won eight in other types of cars, including sports cars and midget cars. His 26 wins since 1999 trail only Jeff Gordon's in that time. Stewart's background in Indy cars, another form of racing, helped him become one of the only drivers to race in the Indy 500 and a NASCAR race on the same day!

Tony Stewart has 26 wins since 1999. He is second only to Jeff Gordon, who has 33.

Jimmie Johnson: Most NASCAR racers are from the South, but Johnson grew up in California. He got his start racing motorcycles and dune buggies in desert races, but switched to tracks and found great success. He won his first NASCAR championship in 2006 after finishing second in 2005.

What's With All the Decals?

Your family car might have a couple of bumper stickers, but NASCAR vehicles do not stop there. They are almost completely covered by colorful decals. Why? One word: money! Every one of the decals on a NASCAR vehicle means money for the team owner. Teams sell sponsorships and use that money to buy equipment and pay employees. In turn, the sponsor's company is advertised on the car.

The more money a sponsor pays, the bigger the decal. Some sponsors buy space on all the cars, while others put all their money muscle behind one driver. You might hear a driver say that his "Dupont Hendrick Motorsports Chevy ran really well today." Every time the sponsor's name is mentioned, it makes it easier for a team to sell—more sponsorships! Drivers get most of the attention, but sponsors are a key part of any NASCAR team.

Matt Kenseth: Kenseth grew up in Wisconsin and started racing on small tracks there. In 2003, he became one of NASCAR's youngest champions by capturing the title when he was only 23 years old.

Dale Earnhardt, Jr., is one of the most popular drivers in NASCAR.

Dale Earnhardt, Jr.: The son of Dale Earnhardt, Sr., was voted by fans as NASCAR's most popular driver three years in a row. Dale, Jr., in the red Number 8 car, has had some success on the track, but not as much as his devoted fans would like to see. He won the Daytona 500 in 2004, but has not yet captured the season title.

Kasey Kahne: This young racer sometimes seems to get as much attention for his good looks as for his driving. But he is a tough, competitive racer who had five wins in his first two seasons (2004 and 2005).

Dale Earnhardt, Sr.

The most famous driver in NASCAR has not been in a race since February 18, 2001. That day, seven-time champion Dale Earnhardt, Sr., was killed during a crash on the last lap of the Daytona 500. Earnhardt's death stunned the NASCAR community. He was beloved by nearly all its fans, both for his success on the track and the hard-charging, bumper-bumping way he had won his titles.

Sadly, such accidents are sometimes a part of NASCAR. Drivers accept the risk while working hard to avoid trouble. Even more safety measures have been added as a result of Earnhardt's crash, from the HANS device to padded walls at some tracks.

Any souvenir featuring the black Number 3 car Dale, Sr., drove remains among the most popular in NASCAR. The legend of "The Man in Black" will never die.

All Kinds of Drivers

In 2007, former Formula One hero Juan Pablo Montoya of Colombia joined NASCAR's top ranks. (Formula One, like the Indy racing league, is a form of "open wheel" racing.) He became one of the few non-Americans ever to drive in NASCAR. Unlike Formula One or Indy open-wheel racing, virtually all NASCAR drivers are Americans. They are also almost all men.

Some women took part in early NASCAR races, but none race today at the highest level. The Busch Series has seen female drivers such as Shawna Robinson, while Deborah Renshaw has driven in the Craftsman Truck Series. This is not to say that women might not reach the highest level in NASCAR. Women participating in the Chase for the Nextel Cup would add even more excitement to the sport.

All of the drivers combine their skills with those of their teammates, and the great cars provided by the team owners. This large group of experts all aim for one thing—go fast and win. At the same time, their journeys around the track thrill millions. Now, let's go racing!

Glossary

air resistance—The force of air on an object (such as a race car) as it moves through the air. The faster the car goes, the more air resistance it has to work against.

chassis—The metal skeleton or frame of a car.

circuit—A series of several related events, such as NASCAR races.

drafting—The racing technique of driving very closely behind another car to cut down on air resistance.

gears—Car parts that work to accelerate (speed up) or slow down a vehicle's engine.

HANS device—Short for head and neck support device, a series of cables and brackets that help keep a driver's head from moving around suddenly in a crash, helping to prevent injury.

horsepower (hp)—A measure of engine performance and power. It compares the power of one horse to what an engine can do. For example, it would take 850 horses to equal the power of an 850-hp engine.

pace car—The car that leads race cars for a certain number of laps around the track to get them all driving at the same speed.

piston—Engine part that moves up and down rapidly to turn a driveshaft that makes a car's wheels turn.

pit—The area next to a racetrack where a car is serviced during a race and where crew members wait.

qualifying lap—A lap around a racetrack that helps determine the starting positions of drivers in a race.

roll cage—A set of steel bars and tubes welded together to create a safe pocket within the car for the driver, especially if the car rolls over.

sponsor—A company or person who provides money for a race team. In return, the company's logo is shown on the car and the driver.

stock car—The type of car used in NASCAR races. Its design is based on a typical passenger car.

Further Reading

Books

Buckley, James, Jr. *Eyewitness NASCAR.* New York: DK Publishing, 2006.

Caldwell, Dave. *Speed Show: How NASCAR Won the Heart of America.* Boston: Kingfisher, 2006.

Kelley, K.C. *Champions of NASCAR.* Pleasantville, NY.: Readers' Digest Children's Books, 2005.

Woods, Bob. *Dirt Track Daredevils: The History of NASCAR.* Chanhassen, MN.: Tradition Books, 2003.

Internet Addresses

http://www.daytona500.com The history of the Daytona 500, and information on other races held at the track.

http://msn.foxsports.com/nascar Broadcasts many of the top NASCAR events.

http://www.nascar.com The official site of NASCAR.

Index